flowers

HARUHITO WAKO AND MASATO KAWAI

CHRONICLE BOOKS
SAN FRANCISCO

First published in the United States in 1998 by Chronicle Books.

First published in Japan in 1994 by Korinsha Press & Co., Ltd., Tokyo, Japan.

Copyright © 1994 by Korinsha Press & Co., Ltd.
All photographs copyright © 1994 by Haruhito Wako
All rights reserved. No part of this book
may be reproduced in any form without written permission from the publisher.

Printed in Japan.

ISBN 0-8118-1936-1

Library of Congress Cataloging-in-Publication Data available.

Book design: Masahide Yoshida
Cover photograph: Haruhito Wako
Cover design: Carole Goodman

Distributed in Canada by
Raincoast Books
8680 Cambie Street
Vancouver, B.C. V6P 6M9

10 9 8 7 6 5 4 3 2 1

Chronicle Books
85 Second Street
San Francisco, California 94105

Web Site: www.chronbooks.com

flowers that will continue to be alive in the eternal light

15

21

27

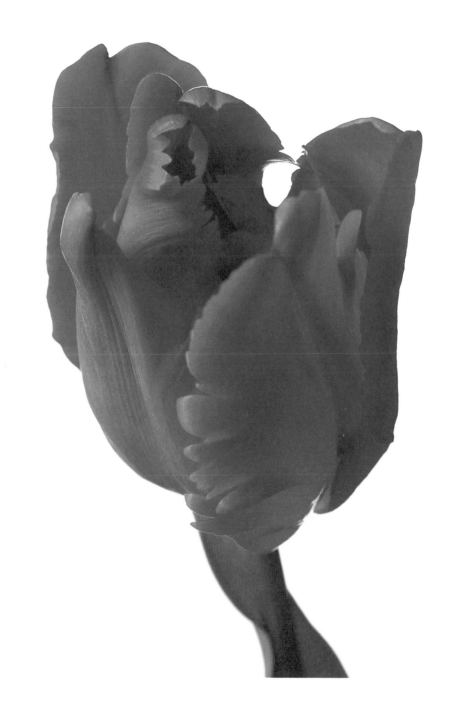

33

39

43

51

57

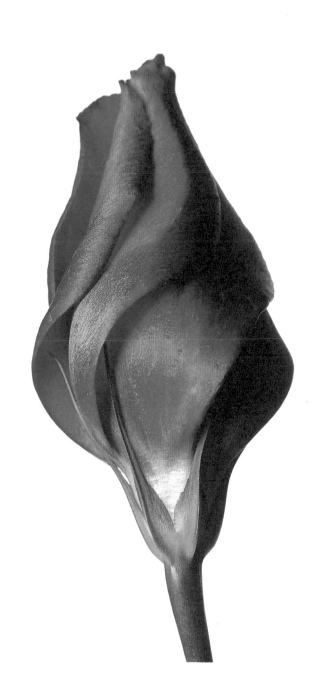

HARUHITO WAKO was born in 1958 in Hokkaido. He studied under Kenji Ishikawa and has had several exhibitions in Tokyo. He is a free-lance photographer who lives and works in Tokyo. *Flowers* is his first book.

MASATO KAWAI was born in Kyoto in 1958. An award-winning flower stylist based in Tokyo, his work has also been the subject of several exhibitions. *Flowers* is his first book.